10-Minute Decorating

10-Minute Decorating

176 Fabulous Shortcuts with Style

Susan Ure

Sterling Publishing Co., Inc. New York
A Sterling/Chapelle Book

Chapelle Ltd.

Owner: Jo Packham

Editor: Linda Orton

Staff: Areta Bingham, Kass Burchett, Marilyn Goff, Holly Hollingsworth, Susan Jorgensen, Kimberly Maw, Barbara Milburn, Karmen Quinney, Leslie Ridenour, Cindy Stoeckl, Gina Swapp, Sara Toliver, Kim Taylor, Kristi Torsak

Photography: Kevin Dilley, for Hazen Imaging, Inc.
Phil Cordova, Cordova Photography
Luciana Pampalone, Luciana Pampalone Studio
Scot Zimmerman for Scot Zimmerman Photography
Joe Coca, Joe Coca Photography

Library of Congress Cataloging-in-Publication

Ure, Susan
   10-minute decorating / Susan Ure.
     p. cm.
   "A Sterling/Chapelle book."
   Includes index.
   ISBN 0-8069-7483-4
    1. Interior decoration. I. Title: Ten minute decorating. II. Title

NK2115 .U73 2001
747--dc21   2001020113

10 9 8 7 6 5 4 3 2 1

A Sterling/Chapelle Book

Published by Sterling Publishing Company, Inc.
387 Park Avenue South, New York, NY 10016
© 2001 by Chapelle Ltd.
Distributed in Canada by Sterling Publishing
% Canadian Manda Group, One Atlantic Avenue, Suite 105
Toronto, Ontario, Canada M6K 3E7
Distributed in Great Britain and Europe by Cassell PLC
Wellington House, 125 Strand, London WC2R 0BB, England
Distributed in Australia by Capricorn Link (Australia) Pty Ltd.
P.O. Box 6651, Baulkham Hills, Business Centre, NSW 2153, Australia
Printed in China
All Rights Reserved

Sterling ISBN 0-8069-7483-4

If you have any questions or comments, please contact:

Chapelle Ltd., Inc.
P.O. Box 9252
Ogden, UT 84409

Phone: (801) 621-2777
FAX: (801) 621-2788
e-mail: chapelle@chapelleltd.com
website: www.chapelleltd.com

Susan Ure was born in Washington state, but has spent the last 30 years as a resident of Salt Lake City, Utah. Her formal training was as a counselor in drug and alcohol rehabilitation. However, in the early nineties her instincts and talents led her to establishing and becoming the proprietress of FLORIBUNDA, a most magical and discerning gift shop in Salt Lake City.

As a young girl, Susan's interests were in rearranging her home. Family members would return from work to find the dining room in the living room, and Susan moving all that was "moveable" from one place to another. Her overall talent for decorating, and more specifically in selecting the perfect piece for any spot and window displays, has inspired family, friends, and customers most of her adult life. Susan has three sons, six grandchildren, and lives with her husband and two dogs in the foothills of the Rocky Mountains.

Dedicated to the memory of my mother
LaRae Strom

Table of Contents

Introduction

With the rush and responsibilities of everyday life, there is rarely enough time or money to redecorate as often as desired. *10-Minute Decorating* shares ideas for decorating, oftentimes with items already on hand. A scarf can be knotted and placed around a free-standing mirror, or a simple floral arrangement may be placed on a china shelf containing a collection of unmatched crystal glassware. Whether one is displaying a collection or a few favored objects, simple rearrangments can be done in a 10-minute or less time frame.

Comprehensive design tips on how to add accents are included for virtually every room in the house. A surplus of ideas for lighting, walls, windows, containers, and much more are shown in full-color photographs. Candles can be mixed and matched, unique fabrics may become table covers, and books stacked artfully allow favorite pieces to be displayed at the last moment before guests arrive. Whatever the decorating style may be—country, "shabby chic," Victorian, or contemporary—ideas can be found for 10-minute decorating.

Chapter 1
Containers

Containers come in such extraordinary styles and materials. Goblets, jars, bowls, and baskets can be filled with contrasting wonders, limited only by the imagination. No matter what the container, it may hold an equally large content variety.

design idea 1
10-minute tip: Fill a vase with feathers in place of flowers.

This bouquet is made up of peacock, ostridge, and pheasant feathers which in turn complement the antique peacock shawl on the wall.

design idea 2
10-minute tip: Tie a tassel to the lid of a decorative jar.

The clear apothecary jar was filled with seashells and allows one to see the many forms within it much better than if they were sitting in a bowl.

design idea 3
10-minute tip: Fill a treasured container with unexpected contents.

This little cement angel came bearing gifts. In the bowl, she holds colored pieces of glass etched with loving thoughts of peace, hope, and joy. An embossed velvet scarf is casually placed about her neck. When she is placed in the bathroom, her bowl may contain bars of soap.

2

3

24

design idea 24
10-minute tip: Use edible objects for containers.

Here, the container happens to be a bread bowl and has a hearty visual effect. A container of water was placed inside a hollowed-out bread bowl and filled with berries, grapes, and a single Gerbera daisy.

design idea 25
10-minute tip: Allow a single container to fill an entire space.

A square window embraces a round container that in turn is filled with layers of brightly colored vegetables.

It may be the container that makes the entire statement for an arrangement or the contents that can be seen within it.

design idea 23
10-minute tip: Place fresh fruit or vegetables into a transparent container, fill with water, and place a floating candle on top.

This is a great example of how the contents become the "magic" of this container. A full view of the raffia-bundled carrots reveals the color and freshness of the vegetables.

25

26

design idea 26

10-minute tip: Use edible items and dishes from the kitchen for arrangements and centerpieces.

The large bowl looks like a "Fall" offering to the hostess of a Thanksgiving dinner and the smaller bowl attractively holds fresh bread for the meal. The African violet is potted in its own container and the vegetables are held in place with florist picks.

design idea 27

10-minute tip: Use the food that you will be serving as part of the table decorations.

These baskets are filled with colorful fresh peppers and a variety of breadsticks, and their contents are easily accessible when preparing or eating a favorite meal.

design idea 28

10-minute tip: Elegant flowers such as roses can be mixed with fruits and vegetables in floral arrangements.

Roses and lilies are snuggled inside this oriental basket along with miniature pumpkins that set the tone with their rich color.

27

29

The smooth surface of the measuring cups against the stucco surface of the windowsill is such a pleasing contrast.

design idea 31
10-minute tip: A picture frame can be used for table displays or place settings.

A plain wooden picture frame encloses an artful display of food. What a wonderful surprise it would be to use an assortment of picture frames to "frame" delicious dishes at a dinner party.

30

design idea 29
10-minute tip: Outdoor planters can be brought indoors for uses other than planters.

Handmade clay-chicken planters are sitting pretty with a rustic wooden door and cuttings of raspberry bushes as a backdrop. The natural look of the containers, combined with painted wooden eggs, berries, and fruit scattered around the table, enhances the country theme.

design idea 30
10-minute tip: Display vegetables from the refrigerator or garden in kitchen utensils and containers.

These French ceramic measuring cups are simple, yet artistic in design. The terra-cotta flowerpot of fresh herbs, asparagus, and tomatoes not only adds color, but also ties into the cooking element.

31

32

Chapter 2

Textiles

Fabrics, scarves, quilts, pillows, and laces are some of the most wonderful decorative details in one's home and take but a moment to arrange.

design idea 32
10-minute tip: Make a quick change by placing a throw or delicate fabric across a bed or over a chair.

A velvet throw was placed on the bed and silk fabric was draped over the chair. It is a great way to change a room seasonally or "just because." Layers of fabric add the quality of warmth during fall and winter. In the spring, a layer or two can be removed.

33

34

design idea 33
10-minute tip: Bring the throws out of the closet and display them on chairs or other furniture.

This straight-backed chair becomes a resting place for a lovely crocheted throw that softens the look of the chair. The chair and throw create a sense of heritage with the antique desk and old family photographs.

design idea 34
10-minute tip: Fabrics can be layered over tables and knotted.

Fabric was draped over this end table. One piece was twisted and wrapped around the table edge, then knotted to create an elegant look. The table is framed from behind with a live palm.

35

36

design idea 36
10-minute tip: Bring wearables out of the closet and display them on sofas and chairs.

Surround yourself with beloved items, such as this shawl that was a gift from a wonderful artist. When the shawl is not being worn, it still can be enjoyed when draped across the back of a chaise.

design idea 37
10-minute tip: Use scraps of fabrics for covering pillows that are in need of a change.

A length of fabric covers the back and seat of this overstuffed chair. The neck-roll pillow is covered with a small piece of satin that was a leftover piece from a duvet cover. Each end was tied with satin cording, and no sewing was necessary.

Pillows can be expensive and not something one would want to replace over and over again.

design idea 35
10-minute tip: Change the look of a pillow by wrapping it with a shawl and tying an attractive knot.

When ready for a change, take a piece of fabric—in this case a sari from Bali—and tie or knot it very simply around the pillow. A fringed silk shawl was arranged behind the pillow and a smaller pouch-style pillow was placed in front to add an Oriental element, integrating this look with the remainder of the room.

37

Pillows, pillows, and more pillows—they are terrific to use when needing a quick decoration fix. The fabric of the pillow can say so much.

design idea 38
10-minute tip: Pillows can be placed as decorative elements in places other than on a chair, sofa, or bed.

The hand-painted tulips on this pillow are charming in combination with the lace background, a porcelain figure, and vintage china. The dark color of the pillow is a nice contrast against the white lace of the hutch.

design idea 39
10-minute tip: Mix patterns and textures in pillows to add interest to simple designs.

38

39

The embroidered ribbon edging and fringe on the tube pillow complement the stripes of the fabric-covered chair, as well as the more elegantly patterned and tasseled square pillow.

design idea 40
10-minute tip: Use decorative elements from old clothing and accessories to embellish pillows.

The black crushed-velvet pillow has antique beads attached from a 1920s' flapper dress. This is a much better way to admire the vintage workmanship than keeping it in the attic in a storage box.

design idea 41
10-minute tip: Make a clean and simple statement by placing one attractive pillow on a chair or sofa.

This high-backed wicker chair would seem rigid and uninviting without this single pillow to cushion you. Even if one has to move the pillow to sit back, its presence beckons a guest to have a seat.

design idea 42
10-minute tip: Bring in outdoor furniture and wrap the cushion or twin-sized mattress in fabric.

Simply designed furniture pieces such as this piece of outdoor furniture could appear to be quite cold and stiff without the fabric-wrapped mattress and a selection of pillows loosely tossed across the cushion and along the back.

41

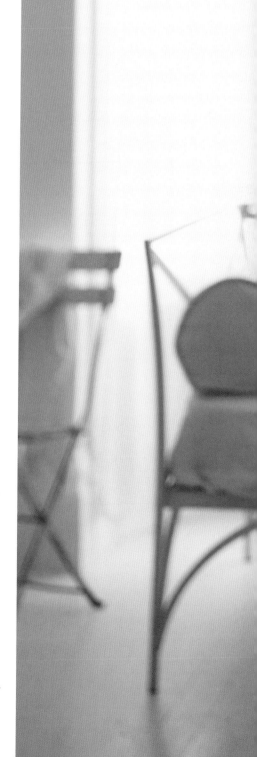

42

Enjoy art in its great variety of forms, and your space will have more history, heritage, and diversity. Not all art hangs on a wall or sits on a table.

design idea 43
10-minute tip: Hang wearables over doors for decorative elements.

These two scarves hung over a door are also wearable art. When they are not being worn, they are used to decorate a door or wall so they can be enjoyed year round.

design idea 44
10-minute tip: Combine various ethnic designs and objects.

The quilt displayed over the wall beam not only draws the eye upwards, but adds an element of art to an otherwise empty space. An unlikley combination is the early American quilt and the Oriental carpet, yet they complement one another and bring continuity and warmth to the room. This room has a minimal amount of accessories such as a single vase on the mantle, but it is this simplicity that allows the quilt and rug to be the primary focus.

44

45

46

design idea 45
10-minute tip: Knot the fringe on tablecloths and table runners.

This table runner was placed on top of a hutch and allowed to hang over the edge, displaying the elegant woven pattern. A painted wooden church and metal candlestand with candle make a lovely arrangement and are a quite different approach from a silk floral planter or basket.

design idea 46
10-minute tip: Ribbons and trims can be hung from a rod to make unique wall hangings.

This ribbon wall hanging accents a corner nook in a more formal setting. A wooden curtain rod is hung on the wall and an assortment of ribbons and trims are cut to graduated lengths and looped over the rod to make a quick and simple wall hanging.

An ivy planter, an old thread spool and wooden cylinders used as candleholders, vintage leather-bound books, and a metal cherub frame containing an old photograph are arranged on the metal filigree and marble end table.

design idea 47
10-minute tip: Drape a vintage scarf and allow it to hang down the side of the surface that it is placed on.

An oversized silk floral arrangement sits on an antique embossed-velvet scarf with beaded fringe. Three decorative bottles complement the arrangement, with a short length of exquisite ribbon knotted around the neck of each bottle.

47

69

design idea 68
10-minute tip: Lace scraps can be used as tiebacks for curtains.

A wide piece of scrap lace is used to tie back a drapery panel. Behind the drapery is a lace curtain that brings together the Victorian theme in this room setting.

design idea 69
10-minute tip: Use a table runner as a window valance.

Everything in its place and a place for everything? Not necessarily. This table runner found a new resting place atop a curtain rod. Lace curtains cover the entire window beneath the table runner, and patterned drapes flank each side.

design idea 70
10-minute tip: Layer two curtains over a window and tie one in a knot.

This knotted curtain would look great on a paned-glass door. This look could be repeated with any fabric and contrasting backdrops.

70

10-minute tip: Tie back curtains with tassels.

A single tassel modestly ties back these floral drapes and is simple to slip off when you need to block out the light. A lace valance covers the curtain rod and outer curtain panel to add a softening touch across the window.

design idea 72
10-minute tip: Use kitchen napkins placed over a curtain rod for valances.

Originality keys this setting. A painted door frame covered with lace panels, floral fabric, and white eyelet napkins catches the eye. A set of curtain rods are hung onto the door below the first set of windowpanes and covered with lace panel curtains. Patterned curtains were placed on a second rod above the top windowpanes and pulled back beyond the door frame with tassels. Freshly ironed kitchen napkins top off the look.

71

73

design idea 74
10-minute tip: Attach a length of fabric to a curtain rod and allow it to swag.

A short wooden curtain rod was attached at one side of the window, rather than across the width of the window. A curtain panel was gathered onto the rod, then a rich fabric with beautiful drape was attached to each end of the rod and allowed to swag below the top of the curtain. This is another variation of how one can play with textiles and try out new and unconventional ways to accent windows.

design idea 73
10-minute tip: Wind a floral garland around a curtain rod.

Valances can be created in a divers number of ways and with a variety of materials. This valance was made by using two lengths of fabric and knotting one end of each length to the curtain rod. Each length was brought to the center of the rod, allowing the fabric to swag. The remaining two ends of the fabric were knotted together to hang from the center of the curtain rod. A garland of silk flowers was then wrapped around the curtain rod and an empty frame was hung over the underlying curtain panels. This window treatment would be used on a window where the draperies are not drawn.

74

75

design idea 75
10-minute tip: Attach fabric to a curtain rod with knots.

The curtain is created with two different lengths and types of fabrics, each tied into a knot at one end and swagged over a glass-block window. A particularly interesting effect is the different lengths of the fabric and the fact that the window treatment is also knotted on the hanging end.

design idea 76
10-minute tip: Tie back curtains with oversized tassels.

A layered effect has been applied to this modest window with a window blind behind the curtain when privacy is needed.

76

77

Chapter 4

Walls

Decorating walls is more than applying paint or wall-paper; it is anything that is placed on them or in front of them.

78

design idea 77
10-minute tip: Hang a shawl or other wearable on the wall in place of framed artwork.

The focal point in this guest room is above the bed where an embroidered silk shawl was hung. Clear push pins were used—rather than a curtain rod—to create the gathered and draped effect with the fringe falling randomly. The fabric falls naturally, as it would if someone was wearing it.

An heirloom piece of lace is draped over the shade on one of the wall-mounted brass lamps. This is an obvious indication of which side of the bed belongs the lady of the house.

design idea 78
10-minute tip: Hang scarves on walls in small spaces.

A silk hand-painted scarf is hung on a narrow wall space next to glass tiles. The small wicker drawers topped with bouquets of ostrich feathers and fresh flowers give a complementary touch to this wall. The feathers repeat the painted motif in the scarf.

10-minute tip: Hang original artwork in the bedroom or less formal areas of the home where it can be enjoyed by those who live there.

Original art need not be experienced in only those rooms where entertaining and guests may visit. A large blank wall in this bedroom is just the place for oversized art. The contemporary style of this room with its relatively unadorned—except for a bold-colored paint—walls becomes the perfect setting for brightly colored original artwork, whether it is hanging on the wall or leaning against the wall in a large alcove at the head of the bed. The alcove also becomes a bookshelf to hold books one would like to read or study during quiet personal times.

79

80

81

82

Picture frames are one way to fill a wall space. How the frames are placed is another matter. Placement can convey formal or informal tones in a room. Balance is a key factor when arranging a group of framed artwork.

design idea 80
10-minute tip: When hanging framed pictures or other objects, try breaking up the pattern with a different shape.

The top of this doorway has a finished look by the way these serving trays are arranged above the doorway. Notice how placing an oval-shaped tray in the middle breaks up the design.

design idea 81
10-minute tip: Group four frames of similar size and shape together with a fifth larger picture placed off to the side.

Four smaller frames are placed together and a larger one just to the right creates a nice balance next to a large lamp.

design idea 82
10-minute tip: Place a row of small picture frames underneath larger framed artwork.

This is a very nontraditional way to group picture frames on the wall. The lamp helps add balance where another frame might ordinarily be placed.

design idea 83
10-minute tip: Group unusually shaped frames together on a wall.

In this collection, frames are made of similar materials, metal and wood, and contain like subject matter; but that is where the similarities end. This eclectic grouping has an Old Spanish feeling in a room that contains ethnic objects on the table and the doorknob. Although the frames are of very different shapes, the setting has a cohesive feeling.

Sometimes one finds a small card or trinket that one simply does not want to live with-out. Instead of having boxes of these treasures put away, try framing them to display their individuality. Here, two gift cards, which have small pieces of tapestry, beads, and

dried lavender, were framed and hung in the bathroom. If one tires of them there, it takes only minutes for them to be relocated somewhere else.

This was a very small and plain bath-room. Everything in the room, including the color, was quiet and subtle. This room needed a spot of bright color or a "color surprise." This oversized print with its bold colors gives the bathroom the dramatic focus and weight that was needed.

Other accessories that brighten and add mood to this monotone bathroom include the orchid and candle sitting on a shelf above the bathtub, along with the elegant shell drawers where another candle sits with assorted shell artifacts.

84

86

design idea 86
10-minute tip: Hang decorative objects between shelves.

Sometimes shelves and walls have enough going on. An unexpected place was found for this whimsical clock on the column between the two sets of shelves.

design idea 87
10-minute tip: Place a picture frame on the couch instead of on the wall.

Being unpredictable is the artist's way! An old picture frame that has been in the family for twenty years contained the photograph of a grandmother's friend. The value to the immediate family was not in the photograph, but in the frame. Some dried flowers from the garden were glued onto a piece of mat board and framed.

87

88

design idea 88
10-minute tip: Allow a piece of art to fill an entire space, such as from the ceiling to the top of the door jamb.

A narrow space above the doorway in the kitchen needed decoration, and although dishes are often the accessory of choice, something different was desired. This lovely, carved wooden art piece from Mexico was the perfect companion to adorn this particular spot.

10-minute tip: Glue buttons onto magnets to secure photographs to metal surfaces

Old buttons glued onto magnets enhance the feeling of age, as well as adding color and ornamentation. Other trinkets could be used in place of buttons.

10-minute tip: Hang an old door on the wall and embellish with photographs.

There were too many picture frames hanging on this dining-room wall, and none of the frames were particularly compatible or interesting. Buying new frames for so many pictures would have been much too costly. Found in the garage was an old screen door that was used in place of the frames. It is a fun way to to display photographs that were previously in frames. To soften the hard edges of the door "frame," a tassel was tossed over one corner of the frame and a piece of old lace was draped over the other. A bouquet of dried roses was attached to the upper edge of the screen. Since the screens were metal, magnets could be used to secure the photographs in place.

89

90

Most people see a blank wall and are intimidated with so much open space. No decision must be final when it comes to decorating walls.

design idea 91
10-minute tip: Decorate a wall with individual calendar pages.

An easy solution was applied to this wall by using manila envelopes which have endearing applications of calendar artwork. The random placement of the envelopes around the corner of the desk adds a playful note to the informal artwork in an otherwise more formal setting.

design idea 92
10-minute tip: Place two colorful leaves on the wall for an element that is in itself, beauty and simplicity.

Two autumn maple leaves are placed just above the desk surface. On a larger scale, the simple lines of this open desk accentuate the detail of the faux-painted wall.

An assortment of objects placed on the desk adorn as well as enhance the large wall space behind it. An orchid brings in nature while a sphere on a pedestal and a finial become bookends. A miniature photograph is framed with an extra wide mat and leans against the wall rather informally. Books are arranged in a wire basket as well as stacked on the desk, stool, and floor.

91

118

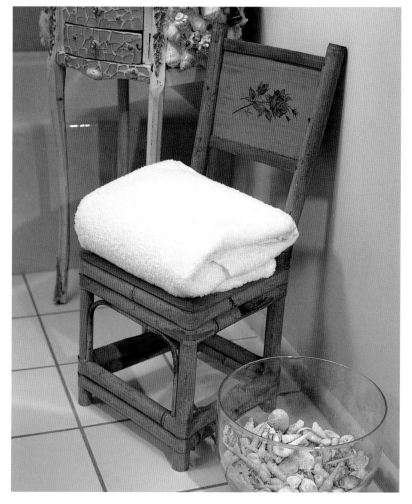

119

An oversized bath towel sitting on a bamboo chair in the guest bath is another way to place ready-to-use items.

A large serving bowl filled with a variety of seashells sits on the floor to one side of the chair, creating an atmosphere of serenity and tranquility.

design idea 120
10-minute tip: Tip a basket or container on its side for an additional storage shelf.

A simple wooden shelf, housing towels within a basket and stacked towels, is only made more thought provoking when the legs to the shelf are actually decorative clay pots. Two unusually shaped bottles and a handthrown clay container are the only other accents in this display of simplicity.

design idea 118
10-minute tip: Use an aged table such as a potting table to hold towels or bedding.

A collection of everyday items, such as soaps and cotton balls in glass containers, and buckets filled with fresh flowers are displayed among the towels on an old potting table, creating an interesting grouping. This display is all about details.

design idea 119
10-minute tip: Use a chair to hold fresh towels in place of a towel rack.

120

Storage is always a challenge when one wants to store the trappings of a hobby or a craft, while still requiring easy access to those items or supplies. Remember that a hobby or craft is an art form and take pleasure in displaying the tools of the craft. Supplies need to be visible and easily accessed when it is time for creative juices to flow.

design idea 121
10-minute tip: Old hutches and cupboards are a creative solution for storing sewing or craft supplies.

This older cabinet is home for sewing supplies such as bobbins of thread, pin cushions, scraps of vintage lace and fabric, and bolts of ribbon. Fabric-covered boxes, glass bottles, and ceramic dishes hold small sewing notions such as buttons and pins. Not only do the sewing supplies find storage in this well-worn cabinet, but they embellish it as well.

design idea 122
10-minute tip: Remove drawers and use as shelves for those hard to store items.

Faux-finished cabinets with the center drawers removed provide storage for an assortment of decorative and handmade papers.

design idea 123
10-minute tip: Old glass showcases or other furniture pieces that are open on top are good storage for wrapping papers.

Additional papers are stored upright in an old glass showcase. These rolls of paper are easily stored where the colors and patterns can be seen at a glance.

122

123

Stacking chairs on chairs, a chair on a side table, pillows in front of pillows, or an oversized mirror on a trunk are great ways to invent a personalized look.

design idea 124
10-minute tip: Stack similar items in graduated sizes.

Stacking chairs on chairs in three graduated sizes is whimsical and somewhat reminiscent of a favorite fairy tale, with a small giftwrapped box placed on the seat of the smallest chair.

125

124

design idea 125
10-minute tip: Use doll furniture as servers on the countertop or at the table.

This miniature red chair, amidst all the blue, ties the framed print and the fresh roses into the room décor. The chair seat offers an additional surface on which to stack a homemade jar of jelly.

design idea 126
10-minute tip: Stack books by color, topic, and size as a decorative element in the study or living room.

The mirror commands dramatic attention while the trunk provides the mirror with a sturdy foundation on which to rest. The velvet pillows stacked on the chair lend harmony to the striped wallpaper, and a small footstool serves as another surface on which to place these favored books.

127

It is not often that one would think to use shoes as a decorative element or accent. It is more common to think that shoes should be put away out of sight. Baby's first pair of shoes may be bronzed or porcelain-covered to preserve them and the memories they evoke.

design idea 127
10-minute tip: Display shoes as if they are an artform.

The simple tilt of the shoe is no accident, but a coy statement of the time period that these shoes represent as well as an artful presentation. Chairs are also oftentimes works of art and this chair is no exception. It is used as a backdrop for this wonderful pair of nineteenth-century shoes and sets an atmosphere of nostalgia. Light flooding through a window covered by sheer white curtains and potted ivy are subtle touches.

128

design idea 128
10-minute tip: This white-on-white ensemble is dramatic, especially with the small touches of color in the fruit and flowers.

129

The white vase with peonies takes the spotlight in this grouping. The green leaves point down, drawing the eye towards the tiny hatbox with a young girl's shoe. The eye is drawn, next, to the perfectly shaped pears in a white bowl. This is a restful and soul-pleasing display of accessories.

design idea 129
10-minute tip: Display sports equipment as a decorative element and in a way that suggests they are ready for use.

A woven-wicker rocker, sitting on a built-in porch tilts back slightly from the weight of old leather ice skates. The casual feeling created here makes one feel welcome as well as inferring the opportunity to indulge when a frozen pond beckons all skaters.

10-minute tip: Use children's toys, antique or new, as a decorating accent.

A pine hutch filled with lace, antique tablecloths, quilts, and a small tea set defines a room for vintage children's toys—or an adult who loves such things. A stocking made from collected pieces of fabric, lace, and ribbon, filled with a handmade teddy bear, adorns the hutch doors the entire year. A larger teddy

bear, dressed in an heirloom christening dress, waits expectantly for a special visitor.

design idea 131
10-minute tip: Display quilts on the wall and framed artwork on a bed or sofa.

This bed has unusual "guests" when two framed needlepoints are placed with the pillows. The idea of a quilt on the wall and frames on the bed is a delight. Hatboxes are stacked to the right of a small round pedestal table, with a miniature lamp and vintage telephone placed upon it. Nothing ordinary in this guest room!

130

131

133

134

design idea 134
10-minute tip: Tie delicate neck scarves around metal objects such as this metal mirror.

The hard metal edges of this unique and freestanding mirror is softened by a neck scarf with a tassel. The lavender bottle and casually placed scarf, sitting on the tabletop, also ease the angles.

design idea 132
10-minute tip: Look for an original use for items other than what they were designed for.

This Chinese serving cabinet is placed in the bathroom to be used for cotton balls, swabs, and other toiletries. A statue of Quin Yin stands where the sewing bobbins would ordinarily be placed. The orchid adds balance and color to the overall setting.

design idea 133
10-minute tip: Create a shelf within a shelf to display miniature objects so they can be more easily seen.

A small shelf within a shelf provides an additional place and allows for a more intimate look at the miniatures, the tagged and labeled bottle collection, and the embellished frames and albums.

135

Chapter 6

Mother Nature

One cannot resist the beauty of nature, whether it is in planting a garden and tending it, or bringing the outdoors inside through flowers—fresh or dried. Bringing nature into the home may also include accents in a sun room, or a planter that is versatile enough to be used either indoors or outdoors.

design idea 135
10-minute tip: Use a chair or bench as a plant stand.

Lilacs and hydrangeas get the seat of honor on this bamboo-backed chair. The color and diversity of real flowers are endless and an effective way to adorn any space.

design idea 136
10-minute tip: Bring outdoor planters indoors and put them to use as a centerpiece.

An array of foliage and flowers is combined in an old and aged clay pot that can be brought inside and used as a centerpiece.

design idea 137
10-minute tip: Embellish plain flowerpots with artificial fruit.

This dried lavender topiary is sitting pretty on a stack of hatboxes. Wire-edged ribbon, artificial fruit, and other dried botanicals were hot-glued onto the terra-cotta flowerpot and topiary.

136

137

138

design idea 163
10-minute tip: Place a table lamp in front of a mirror to reflect the lamplight.

The small lamp brightens the walkway in this entry where it sits low to the ground. The lamp also highlights the decorative accessories beside it, as well as reflecting light off the mirror behind it. Notice the small vases that have been placed on the floor on either side of the table.

design idea 164
10-minute tip: Place a standing lamp next to a small table to highlight the accessories placed upon it.

This hand-painted lamp shade rests on a copper and pewter lamp stand, which in turn accents the silver-leafed table and vases on it. The pattern in the lamp shade has a leaf design that complements the other florals in the room. The lamp highlights a beautiful table and the floral placed upon it.

design idea 165
10-minute tip: Tack a beaded necklace or choker around a lamp shade.

A lamp fixture and silk shade trimmed with beads points upward instead of down, and the warm glow of light softens the ambiance in this room. By turning the fixture upward, it does not interfere with the potted orchid sitting directly below it.

164

165

167

168

design idea 167
10-minute tip: Age a paper parasol by tearing pieces from the ribs.

One parasol was torn to suggest a weathered atmosphere and to create interest.

design idea 168
10-minute tip: Hang paper parasols from the ceiling.

By mixing color, patterns, and a few torn parasols, a mosaic effect was fashioned among the rafters that is unexpected, but well worth noticing. The light filtering through the tissue illuminates the parasols' designs and is an added bonus that is also cost effective.

design idea 166
10-minute tip: Tack and drape a wearable or a length of fabric to the ceiling.

Parasols filter light and draw the eye away from the unsightly pipes and track lighting in this room. Between the collection of paper parasols, a Sari is attached to the ceiling and draped. Each parasol is hung with a colorful ribbon.

169

design idea 169
10-minute tip: Place a lamp on a low surface and allow the light to radiate upward.

Not all light has to come from above eye level. This tall table lamp is perfect for a low Chinese-style side table. The gentle spiral of the silk shade is a dramatic design element that looks great, whether it is lit or not. The message that comes from the combination of the lamp, the chinese side table, and a chair that has been covered with various patterns and textures of fabric is that furnishings and accessories need not come from the same time period or style.

design idea 170
10-minute tip: Drape strings of beads around a chandelier.

Lamp shades can change a chandelier at once. Formal silk shades may add drama, whereas these beaded shades suit this gypsy chandelier. Strings of beads were draped and looped around the lamp fixture. The brass chandelier was purchased from a local thrift store.

170

10-minute tip: Mix and match candlesticks on the buffet or dining table.

Three different styles of crystal candlesticks reflect the light from the nearby window. The candlelight reflects against the windowpane, creating a play of natural light and firelight. The candlesticks allow the sunlight to filter through and refract off the cut glass.

171

design idea 172
10-minute tip: Display candlesticks on a bar tray with other bar accessories.

Here, the candlelight and candlesticks sitting on a bar tray are duplicated by a mirror hung on the wall. This is a crystal and glass combination resembling ice touched by the warmth of candlelight and reflected back into the room. The glass vase of fresh florals also adds a touch of warmth and life.

design idea 173
10-minute tip: Float candles and blossoms in a shallow serving dish.

Floating candles, combined with sprigs of fresh flowers, are an inviting sight in any bathroom or entry. The combination of fire and water creates a contrast that is pleasing to the senses. A clear bowl was used in this arrangement, but any type of container, ceramic, metal, or clay, could be used, depending upon the environment that one desires to create.

design idea 174
10-minute tip: Create an arrangement with candlesticks and florals.

The single white rose floating in a crystal cup and the cala lillies nestled in among these lighted candlesticks bring together a cooling effect from the flowers to the fire element.

design idea 175
10-minute tip: Make floating candleholders from drinking glasses.

Colored sea glass and fresh herbs in water, topped with a floating candle, can light up any kitchen counter with a refreshing natural look. The color combinations brighten the glass and can be customized to suit any kitchen or dining area.

174

175

10-minute tip: Place tiki torches into a floral arrangement.

A sense of opulence is created
for indoors or out, when
Hawaiian florals are combined
with tiki torches. The concept
of placing candles among
flowers may not be so new
and unique, except that the
torches stand three feet tall.
Try something new and daring
when decorating with lighting.

176

Index

Acknowledgments

The publishers wish to thank the following for the use of their projects, homes, businesses, or photographs:

Susan Alexander and Taffnie Bogart: pp 24(t)(b), 25, 30

Vanessa-Ann: pp 13(u), 33(u), 45, 46(b), 48, 49(u)(l), 50, 51, 52, 55, 78, 80, 111(b), 122, 129

Corbis Corporation Images (©2000): pp 12, 18, 20, 26, 31(u), 36(b), 38(b), 38–39, 79, 95, 120(b), 140, 141(b)

Anita Louise Crane: pp 23(b), 36(u), 60, 61(u), 62, 64, 100, 106

Diana Dunkley: pp 33(b), 42(u)(b), 43, 88(m)

Linda Durbano: pp 59(u), 61(u), 63, 64(u)(l), 65(u)(r)

Mary Jo Hiney: p 89

Chris Larkin: pp 1, 11(b), 138

Luciana Pampalone: pp 83, 104, 105(u)(b), 110, 111(t), 114(b), 116–117, 117(t), 118(u)(b), 119

Photodisc, Inc. Images (© 1995, 2000): pp 27(b), 31(b), 94, 120–121

Jo Packham: pp 40, 67, 80, 88, 90(u)(b), 96(u)

Robert Perron: pp 41, 70(u)(m)(b), 71

Pat Poce: pp 9(u), 14(u)(b), 15, 19, 22, 23(t), 27(u), 28(u)(b), 29, 44, 102(u), 114(u(b), 115, 123, 132, 139, 141(u), 142

Rhonda Rainey: p 133(u)

Edie Stockstil: pp 46(u), 86, 87(u)(b), 88(u), 124, 125(l)

Scot Zimmerman: pp 52, 68–69

GAYLORD S